ONCE-JOINED PIECES
MEMOONA AHMED

First published in the United Kingdom in 2023.
© Memoona Ahmed 2023
The poet has asserted their right under the Copyright,
Designs and Patents Act, 1988 to be identified as the author
of their work.

All rights reserved.

This book or any portion thereof may not be reproduced or
used in any manner whatsoever without the express written
permission of the publisher except for the use of brief
quotations in a book review.
First published in the United Kingdom in 2023
by Bite Poetry Press.

www.bitepress.co.uk

ISBN 978-1-915787-55-2

First Edition

Cover photography by Gerard Winter-Hughes

Design by Gerard Winter-Hughes
www.gerardhughes.co.uk

Printed and bound in the UK by Biddles, Castle House East
Winch Road, King's Lynn PE32 1SF

CONTENTS

I was young **9**
    story 12
    wings 13
    facial lacerations 13
    girls with combs 14
    phantom 15
    special 16
    audition 18
    I met my little brother on 31st March 2011 19
    larceny 20
    a dream is a wish a child wastes 22
    safe 23

I was glue **27**
    shoulders 28
    what's in a name? 29
    displace 30
    hunger 33
    marionette 34
    peacekeeper 36
    totem 37
    motion sickness 38
    unforgivable 39
    she is such a good girl 40
    do not carry me across mud and tar 41
    seeds 43

I was piece **47**
    oath 49
    eleven 50
    distance 52
    nightmare 53
    scrap 54
    sandcastle 55
    pencil shavings 56
    dissolution 57
    self-hurting 59
    the ants and their sun 60
    swing 62
    bedroom 64

cosm(et)ic procedures 67
and everything..69
I was blue 71
basin 73
blue..74
heartbreak on the telephone 75
things I learned when you left...........................76
brushing...79
dive..80
deadfoot...84
say something..85
haunt me subtly 88
once-joined pieces...89
it would be easier if I knew I didn't matter.......91
dry 92
destroy me 93
Dadiamma 94
chronicity...97
I was fish...101
trying 103
hope is 104
waiting...105
what do my eyes look like behind the lids? 107
my sorry bed..109
hoarder...112
forgetting, for some time.................................113
remembering 116
show me the sky 118
guilt 120
waiting room 121
I have to let him down.....................................123
fish on a line 124
grief 126
I am boat...129
onward...131
blank spaces 132
horizon...134
I'm not sorry I married the wind.....................135

swim 136
Bournemouth...137
recompense...138
sister 141
the robin 142
Billie..143
tilted heads 145
imperfect women...147
you..150
bungalow 152
Ta-hi-ti...159
stationary 161
passage 163
escalator girl...164
window sill...166
Acknowledgements 171

8 ONCE-JOINED PIECES

I was young

10 ONCE-JOINED PIECES

story

pass my invites to
the dance class running upstairs
aapi, I'll show you
*

there's a letter in
your pillow mama. today
I wrote a story
*

you are going to be
a star, but the stars were there
only in her eyes

wings

my fairy wings were always tucked
away in the gap behind my bedroom cupboard
to keep the spiders and the moths company;
cheap, plastic things
but the most wonderful treat
to slip my arms through those tatty strings
and become someone entirely not me.
I'd flutter to breakfast, lunch and dinner,
shake my pigtails in the glitter,
wave my knitting needle wand
and it wouldn't matter who believed.
So when they disappeared from their spot
in the dust,
I lost the person inhabiting them.
The spark that seemed to keep me alive
vanished and in turn I
never looked for it.

facial lacerations

I was such a careful child
so it was always an unexpected delight,
those few times injury was physical.
A paper slice from turning pages too hungrily;
scabby knees from the playground;
facial lacs from the tarmac;
the sting of palm against cheek reverberating
and occasionally, bumping heads.
The sight of blood was almost amorous -
so rare, there might as well have been orange juice pumping
through my veins.
It was always with morbid fascination that I asked
"How did you do that?"
Pointers for how to get a crutch to lean on:
friends who would dote.
To this day I have never broken a bone.
Maybe the world's way of compensating
for other injuries, unwanted ones.

girls with combs

I should've smiled like the teeth of that comb
that day when leaving home,
down our main corridor the dim light
catching on my milky whites.
Perhaps the door would have stayed closed
and the house would not have grown walls
taller than a Rapunzel tower,
new traumas on the hour
and true enough, perhaps she would know
when I hugged it to my chest,
screamed when she left,
to not lock doors:
lesson learnt.
Girls with combs live behind them.

phantom

I was playing every role in the play
and now I barely remember anything.
I never did enjoy games I could not win -
and so goes the game of remembering.
My mind seizes, yet my heart aches
to sidle up to my mother's bed in the night,
escaping terrors, even then,
I read out loud because I did not know how to keep words
inside,
then.

My body remembers lightness
only now that it's heavy
and I feel loud and outspoken,
begrudgingly funny,
grumpy and obstinate,
delighting in running.
At least that's how I look in the albums -
phantom actress, waterfall bunches
up to my ribs and a smile as wicked
as a changeling child;
all manner of faces I showed to the world.

The darkness has me wondering
if that girl was me, if I existed -
I remember toys and books
but never feelings,
never meanings
of how she marries with what I am now
and how fairy wings just vanish -
no face to be found.

special

Why couldn't I be anyone's favourite,
I thought as my brother went through to the therapy room.
In reception with the books and the fishes,
I was a rotten thing.
The children's hospital for the sick children,
yes, I know.
Why couldn't I be a sick child?
All I got was the rocking horse.
He was doing hydrotherapy laps
whilst I excavated a book I hadn't read before.

When he was in for his Botox,
I watched films and doodled -
sauntered round the ward and wondered how it would feel
to be put to sleep by mysterious gas
and wake up with my arm in a cast.
Why couldn't I be the one the nurses loved?
(I said hi to them more than enough.)
So brave, so good -
I itched and chewed
but whatever he went through,
he laughed.

His wheelchair was special -
his helmet was special,
his splints were special
and his walker was, well.
My brother was the darling of the playground,
of every doctor's office -
his TAs filled diaries about his daily habits.
His lunches were cut up and always his favourite
and at college he cooked dinners and learned to ride horses.

16 ONCE-JOINED PIECES

He'd always be the favourite,
I thought for a time.
But it was true, I guess,
he'd chase me like a cat,
steal my food, see how I'd react,
laugh louder than a foghorn,
point me out in the hall,
write beautiful cards,
hold my hand on the roads.
He was a toddler when he got my name wrong,
but I was his favourite - Mena just kind of stuck.

audition

I wonder if I had not made that choice -
would I ever have known what it could be
to fly? If I had not opened my mouth
and let out the song, could I have been whole?
Good for something just mine, how right the words
tasted, how crushing the failing force of
gravity in pulling me down. I knew
there was a chance; I knew I could be found.
Like a moth to a flame, or a bee to
its nectar, like a penny-wish turning
over and over before it arches
into the fountain; this was a different
kind of falling. Falling into the stars -
and to think, I almost never wished it.

I met my little brother on 31st March 2011

When I first held him in my arms
I swore I'd protect him like nothing else.
Head full of dark long hair,
he was a wriggly soft thing -
my little beaver
come home to the dam.
I'd fight for him, I decided.
I'd bare my teeth.

larceny

she wept and wept,
I could hear her on the phone
and I wondered how someone could ever be so hurt.
they were patient with her.
their tears were unfathomable to me -
pain for her? despair, for her?

wrenching, throat-tearing sounds
making empty, meaningless threats
to fill the air with something other than her breaths -
her breaths were laboured, sinking underwater stridor;
she would drown no sailors with her song -
they would take one look at her and cast a net
for her scream sounded to the heavens.
she begged to be taken,
and I listened in terror.

hushed whispers - she's broken,
she'll go mad if she carries on this way,
tell her it will be alright, to trust,
to know that she was loved harder
than the ocean could ever drag her under.
I counted every oath, tumbling true from their throats,
every time they paid more to keep her on the phone,
taking stock of my resentment as it rose,
burning fiercer than her heart burning away.

I was hungry, oh yes
I had a penchant for words
and none of them I heard that night
were ones from a story,

from something that made sense.
she had stolen happy endings and ice
pickaxed with her woe
from my childhood home

and I could attest;
her theft had me cross-examine
what they had kept in their store -
it should have been mine.
She stole what was mine -
she found the ship in the night.

oh, the crime was fatal,
it did not register then.
but years and years later
I remembered what she'd taken
in her larcenous grief,
yet no single thief
snatched the piece from my hands,
left an emptiness in my rage
and with my stomach roaring,
I did not care for my age
when I cut the phone lines
and let the ice back in.

ONCE-JOINED PIECES 21

a dream is a wish a child wastes

On its stone lip we sat our elbows bare.
So modest, to hold what we were to entrust it with
in our endless garden,
in the brambled thicket,
at home with our hubris
and adamance,
we'd ask you -

who could caress the end but a child with a coin in his palm?
the names of faraway places magical words on his tongue;
rough-hewn moonstones, eyes jagged whorls of time;
dreaming of spires tall as the cracks on his spine.

With every dime in the cauldron, we conspired for tsunamis,
pale opal sun rising through those lips,
teeth of our eyes glimmering at its sides,
ardent for rain with
celestine weight in descent
to bring us closer,
ever closer -
arms dug into ancient cementings,
heads tipped on our chins,
counting the wishes
as they buoyed the trembling surface
closer
to its end.

safe

Safety is the cassette player at bedtime
reading us the story -
we know all the words, the number of
seconds between the end of the last syllable and the
CLICK.

Safety is a milk moustache and ox horn
antennas:
biscuits, thrifting.
Pastel clips and baby-born fits;
safety is paper and glitter that sticks.

Safety is the dinner lady's golden retriever,
half-blind and aged but he barks when he sees us.
Mama holds my hand (she's scared of dogs).
I grin toothy and wide
because now I am strong.

Safety follows to the classroom,
to the book corner before it's ruined,
my best friend racing me
for the morning task
and the glory of The Sticker.

Safety rings in my ears like hymns in assembly:
a concurrent drone, backing singers.
My brother on his chair
the only one who matches me;
everyone knows we don't sing quietly.

Safety lays a blanket of snow around me
as I coat-sledge downhill,
make angels 'til I've had my fill.
Ice-burn my hands to build Mr Snowman:
warm milk when it doesn't go to plan.

ONCE-JOINED PIECES 23

Safety is a safari with the windows rolled down,
letting the monkeys swing round
and the giraffes stoop low with their black tongues.
Chin on my hands, I smile at the lions
as they pretend to sleep.

Safety is the red swing at my Nana's house
hanging in the middle of the courtyard.
I laugh at his calls to be careful,
head tipping back to the Lahore sky
and diving into air that tastes light.

Safety is Clifton Beach in Karachi
at night in mid-August,
camel-rides and popcorn and losing a slipper:
Sea View is ebony, serene
brushstrokes on midnight paper.

Safety is the moment
just before,
just in my senses.
Booster back seats
and low wooden fences -

safety finds a loophole,
even when I'm in motion;
I am safe.
Swing, bark, grin,
click, stick, sing

the words of the Indian Ocean
to the sailors setting off on the waves.
Safety is,
and it is
and it is

until

24 ONCE-JOINED PIECES

ONCE-JOINED PIECES **25**

26 ONCE-JOINED PIECES

I was glue

shoulders

did I just wake up
one day, having shed my skin,
sleeping in a shell?
*

pin me paper-board
style, watch me carry it all
whilst you feed the plants
*

she can see angels
on my shoulders, she does not
see the rest of it

what's in a name?

When they named me
they put pieces of paper in a plastic bowl
on my Dadiamma's floor.
Three times, the same fold
and fortune be told
the fortunate girl was born.

Fortune is a funny thing
in comparison to fate.
Fickle where fate lies firm,
fortunes can falter and flux
and find no confine in a name.

The antithesis was amusing,
but I held myself together for it had to mean
that there was a real story coming
to live up to,
that when I apologised for what I did,
it was just a farce we were living in,
that this is what princesses do
just before fortune favours them.

displace

I remember the ravines -
deep down into the earth they were.
Such ants on the craters
we carried it all
over.
Hooded by woods,
trees that hung low -
dirt under my nails,
exhaustion even in this liminal space,
tipping my chin to the pockets of grey
through the leaves
as my younger brother hung on to my
weightless limbs.
Branches reaching out to the Other:
this distal place my father knew.

I do not remember us failing,
even crossing the great river
whose volition
terrified me
yet it bore us - my older brother flanked
with a parent on each side in the water.
They did not know how to swim
but for him they tread.
I ran my hand through the foam
and whispered a thank you
and turned ahead
through fields of washing lines,
our backpacks intact,
we walked.
I did not break,

I did not falter
though I know that my lips were cracked and parched -
tearing and drying, tearing and drying -
they all cried, and fought, and I built the tents.
My silence reverberates in my mind still.
Where we were to escape, I imagined towering spires and
domes,
marble and clean pavements.
I would walk down the centre of the road
and close my eyes:
home.

We caught a train somewhere along that allowed our feet to
know
their agony.
The boys slept on my shoulders
and I watched out of the window
for the Other place.
I saw trees and fields,
Masjids cradled by hills and walled villages -
I hungered to jump at every stop,
but there was a collective destination
and I was there on the Journey.
At the end of the line, some indeterminate distance
away from the sun-baked streets and sapphire ocean we had
left,
we dismounted to a wasteland:
a city of crumbling tower blocks,
sepia clouds low mixing with dust.
Through our fading layers and vinegared eyes
we stood in shock

as planes flew overhead;
the stench of rubble invaded our senses
and our hands were empty.

I do not remember how it was that we returned.
I remember only that there were tears on my face
in that ravine
and so desperately I longed for the branch to break,
for the last thing I saw to be the canopy of grey and green.
but they needed me
for the possibility,
however minute,
that our house still stood -
that danger had gone for good.
I clutched the earth in my fists
and dragged
all the trees with all their roots
to bed one day, as secrets should,
in soil claimed
for my Other woods.

hunger

Circlet of coals on my bare stomach -
know what it is to be heavy,
know what it is to be warm
when friendly fire becomes rapid,
drilling against him,
against me
and the waistband centers
whilst I survey
who it is I must fight for this time,
who it is I must be now,
which drought deserves quenching
for if burning myself blue enough
is what it takes
for hunger to dissipate
I will do it.

marionette

the warmth of the yellow spot on my face
made me forget the crowd,
the anxiety,
the crappy costume.
there were no strings - just me:
brooding, goth-girl lover,
nothing special,
but nothing insignificant.
the breaktime piano rehearsals,
the lines that rolled off my tongue in my sleep -
it was a one-way street,
that stage and me
in that little hall with the blue floor
I could've lived a lifetime
building the resistance,
but I didn't.

when we bowed and there was applause,
I looked up and I saw threads
like the ones coming off my dress -
they tugged and I bowed,
short and sharp;
they yanked and I stumbled
flushing hard;
I was a rockstar
snapping my mouth shut,
stiffening up,
ducking back
somewhere behind the yellow
on my Andy Pandy mast:
little brown year six,

prescription one and two fifths,
belly out, throat numb,
blending in, sore as a thumb,
coat-tail girl, on her brother's wings,
stomach thick as Friday pudding,
three rows in catch two smiles thin
and yeah,
winning was fleeting.
But I
had to be me again.

peacekeeper

When I sleep,
wars break out -
artillery and missiles
raining down as the fire on Mars burns.

The moment breath slows
and the world has become secondary -
the ozone is breached,
my brothers run screaming

from the froth of red that spills across the sky.
The rivers that we knew were there
but in waking deny:
we are the only ones that matter.

My loss is keen for though I am at peace,
the grass is not green,
the cows do not graze
and milk does not quench

their thirst - battle comes first
in eyes that turned constellations
into storms landing in my hands.
Rouse me, the warrior

at fifteen who sees skeletons in her dreams,
to fight skeletons in the light of day
so that history may not rewrite itself
in poetic refrains. It rains

when I sleep;
my weapons wet and futile
as my breaths as they shake, yet it is me they awake
hoping for doomsday to end.

totem

They hold me within an inch,
      my toes brushing the earth
as I stare into headlights
      and oncoming traffic veers its course.

            They keep missing.

               We didn't even run a red light, back then -
                  now I run them all the time,
                     pack heat every line
                     yet they keep missing.

Sometimes I wonder if their tin needs oiling:
whether it's just rust.
Tin man didn't need a heart to have
the biggest one,
      so I don't scream
      and I don't squirm,
despite the pain as it ravages me.

               Burning necklace taut -
            I hang benumbed
               and unable, perhaps even if
            I had words -
                  to tell them it's
            okay.

motion sickness

They call it mixed messages, in my lingo;
potty training or disaster-proofing?
Choose one. No, choose all.
No, choose one.
Shunt across the aeroplane aisle
like a drunken sailor,
hoping some kindly stranger
takes pity -
answers can stow away like tray tables,
who knows who might have them?
First-class passionfruit cocktail
of emotions, with a little umbrella
of in-flight entertainment:
down it.
Distraction, distraction, distraction
from the confusion;
what does she want?
What does it mean?
I could make it, you know,
if I jumped.
I don't know whether it would help
or make things worse.

unforgivable

I love her in that unforgivable way.
Dark night on a dark moor:
running.
It stumbles and groans,
too full and it spills
to the grass where
it swells,
finding dew and holding fast
'til there is a river
and she sails away.

I love her in that unforgivable way.
From a mother to a mother,
I have killed my darlings for her.
Cedarwood coffins in the water,
carrying ashen butterfly bodies, long-running limbs,
voiceboxes like offerings shrouded
in velvet.

Led to rest in a castle of steel,
whilst my river flows in pursuit.
Crimes high, and mighty too
just to know the place she has gone to;
we stretch
and meander
and open our mouth wide -
but when we find the ocean
and she does not keep me,
my tears distil
on the moor
where she left me.
I did it all, and I gave all away,
but then, I was always
unforgivable.

ONCE-JOINED PIECES 39

she is such a good girl

Holes -
six feet deep
on the surface of the moon.
Link hands and gaze, up
where innocence starts and ends
in one short voyage
across the tides,
point your finger from afar
as if pearls do not dissolve
in vinegar.

You may pander outside craters,
starved in the plains
of galactic tundra desert;
you won't find your way.
Find perhaps, romance in a warzone, decrepit
in the hollows of the valleys
and the yawning of the chasms,
in the way it magnetises,
clinches to a rhythm
despite no return.
Peer into every grave, though,
and find that those shelves
hold no mystery.
They are just dug for a moon
to its Earth
to be beautiful.

do not carry me across mud and tar

I wrote one day -
I decided:
carrying the memory of me
will be so much lighter than carrying me.

For we carried our foremothers
and look what happened then -
they snagged, they lived like rotten curtains
bearing down on daylight.
They gossiped, in their joint family home
in Kairana -
slept outside, one of them;
cruel eyes, one of them;
better sons, one of them -
swept up zealous in this pastime
and we chose to carry them.

We chose to carry what they did,
the children that they bore
and the settlings of the scores
between wronged and wrong more
poured thick like tar
on the road to Pakistan -
we carried them, and the sores became ours.

Of a prince doomed to live in the dirt
and a wife not cooking for her husband,
of hate festering under table-wood
and veils on heads in the living room -

and I wrote for I knew

ONCE-JOINED PIECES 41

they would hold me like that -
like ashes in a tomb,
resenting how I swallowed light
and failed to take sides,
threading them together
in a knot that they could not untangle
even if by some miracle
they wanted to.

Bad blood - still mud
running between us and the partition,
I will cleave it free of me.
I will knot them, but only them
and glue my lips together
that my children if I ever grow arms to carry them
will never know that the doors
between that house
and ours
were locked shut -
bolts
we were to carry.

seeds

I sit
with hands so empty
the great valleys of the Himalayas
could set stock by them.

What do I hold now?
The cushion against my face,
shuddering as my fortunes change -

gentle anger,
betraying nothing. I am threads,
she says - I must do it.

So I climb, seed in soil
sprouting shame in my lungs,
knocking on his door -

'I'm sorry.' I mouse at the ground.
He nods, placid and I
sit down, thick with derision.

As I read to him,
stagnant, I wonder now
if seeds return to dust?

I wonder if empty hands
are made for bracing
and if emptiness can ever be filled?

Not a word satisfies.
not one of them heals,

ONCE-JOINED PIECES 43

Instead, a new world order

reaches its roots inside of me
and quickly, it pulls.
I'm a farmer; I till soil after all.

ONCE-JOINED PIECES **45**

46 ONCE-JOINED PIECES

I was piece

48 ONCE-JOINED PIECES

oath

My breath stayed in that
corridor of hooks.
There was no after.
*

Tear a sure oath from
your soul when you promise me;
I won't give it back.
*

Before I knew it,
it was over and done with.
I blinked and missed it.

eleven

I knew something was missing
behind the recycle bins
when I called my mother
and she didn't pick up.
There was a tug in my throat;
arrhythmic thunderclaps
against my ribcage,
stomach beginning to digest itself
in preparation.
The pebbles were rocks
in the car park -
buildings of painted steel
towered around me as I fought the urge
to pee my school trousers,
be late to post-break period.
Burning behind my eyes I contemplated
my options
and I did not know
why they were looking at me
as they passed;
I thought this was reasonable
despite the discomfort.
Crying in line at the door,
lying down in the first aid room,
piercing in my gut.
They were hot tears, forehead
stretched like an animal howling
to the moon
to hear its pain.

Everything is everything at eleven.
The world is cut out neatly
in felt and thread,

no snags in the fabric.
There is a full
picture -
the one you understand:
blonde hair and pencil cases,
crushing on celebrities,
partner-up activities,
silence in the misery
and it falls apart
as eternity passes.
You find fragments
and clues - the veil thins
and you curse what you did
and who you became.

When I close my eyes and feel
that haunting, reminiscent feeling
from behind the bins
and the horrors therein,
I remember that I was afraid -
deathly,
that if that phone did not ring
the sky would fall in
and flattened against tarmac
the misery would win,
but in my growing shoes I know,
it was I that was missing
from the felt-glue world
and beyond all else
I embellished in wishes,
I just needed to know
I existed.

ONCE-JOINED PIECES 51

distance

An island on the bottomless ocean,
carved earthquakes blunt with a butcher's blade.
In time and waters, drowned in the garden,
that shrivelled and blackened and early decayed.
The trees, once tall and proud, abandoned hope
for their roots could no longer find the land.
Old and new waste lined her misty-faced coast,
shard-shrewd hearts scattered across her pale sands.
Her letter-winged kite searches the remains
still. For storm after storm that she weathers,
sunny promise then thundering refrain,
she rises yet to catch its shaken feathers.
The sky may tremble, one day seas may shift,
but no closer will the island ever drift.

nightmare

during the trauma,
we placate ourselves with the notion
that it's just a bad dream.
how could it be real?
there aren't words or conscious thoughts
that could describe it.
so logically - we take something beyond comprehension
and turn it into something that makes sense.
but afterwards
in the days,
the months,
the years that follow -
the nightmare is what we turn against
for dream or not
we will always fear
that one day,
we will wake up.

scrap

Bread and butter,
alone by the classroom;
you do it to be sure
no one can find you
and make you feel
something.
Uncovered,
uncharted, untethered
change keying through your pocket
for the novelty of scraps.
Crike for crumbs,
get something down you
before you pitch and strike out
for the thousandth time
and they follow you to the staircase
just until the turn.

sandcastle

I hold my plastic trowel in my little fist, and
build a castle whilst everything else falls down.
There is a great mass in the middle, damp
and around the sides there is a deep moat
to keep the enemies out and the prisoners in.
I dig this circle so many times I lose count.
Then it occurs to me that moats should have water –
I can't leave it empty. That would be too easy.
So I grab my bucket, ignore the voices
and run to the shore, deep enough to fill it,
far back enough that no-one will come running after me.
I return to slosh the frothy ocean water into my moat.
The sand absorbs, only becoming sludge.
I will need more. I run back to the water, just as it recedes.
I will have to wait for another wave.
I fill up again, and add it to the trench, which has started to
dry.
I need to speed this up. A bright idea hits me –
I open one wall of the moat, drawing a line to the tide,
my hands hurt now but I have to finish this.
It will be time to go home soon, and I can't leave my castle
unguarded.
No-one understands the importance like I do.
When I've finished, I put my wet hands on my hips and
survey
the masterpiece. It could do with a few more towers
and lots more shells. But I did my best.
I hope they've all stopped arguing now.

pencil shavings

You know the way a pencil looks sharp
and new as soon as you shave away all
the smudged, blunt bits?
It looks clean and works perfectly
but a fraction of an inch smaller
and you sharpen and sharpen it
and it carries on working,
getting smaller and smaller
but in perfect working condition
until that moment when you realise you
can't sharpen it any further.
It doesn't sit on your thumb and index anymore.
It's impossible to continue with it
and you keep it in your pencil case anyway
just in case
but you never use that pencil again.
It's off the shelf:
no longer worth effort.
It never dies
but it never lives again either.

dissolution

It is this, that I fear,
that I have been warning for months.
When I saw storm clouds that
loomed fearsome,
my tongue was sharp,
pinning notices to walls,
to each who would divert
I pressed papers to palms;
talking me down
for it is just fear
until it comes.

That itching in my fingertips -
they were always ready to fasten
hooks, buttons and buckles,
laces on duffels,
yet I let the mongers of non-fear
loosen my mettles
and I put them to work in other endeavours.
Walking the knife edge:
the stretch of track just before the finishing line
in my sack when I was seven.
Falling short, and always hard.
These bones were not built for that storm.

Yet I dragged down the grass
with intention, with ask
and I stood on the mound when the clouds came
like I knew they would.
With acid rain
down melted the hill.

ONCE-JOINED PIECES 57

the track,
the will,
yet as punishment for my gamble,
bleached blue I am
still.
Dissolution of the world
was never what I was afraid of
It was this.

self-hurting

maybe I do it because
out of the millions
of bruises and batterings
living like parasites invisible
on my body,
this is the only one
I can put a plaster on.

the ants and their sun

she scatters the deliverance
from her pale mustard pall
through veils and smoke
like spot-beams on ants
loafing their way home
praying to lose their load
penance is tall
in a being so small
endeavours of business
and no-one to call
she makes holes where they were not
there before
she mocks and inflicts
she is friend to all
they look on her when warm
curse her futility in the cold
close their eyes to be closer
raise their hands in a plea
take us with you
take us away from here
she plays cat and mouse
a woman with vengeance
in her smile
and all the while
we clamour for the shreds
but shreds will not make
the leaves on our backs
green again
so as she laughs in our wake
the home we built when we were young
crumbles to ash and dust

and dries the tears
as they fall on the earth
the earth where once
we were to grow.

swing

There is more than one type of freedom on a park swing.
The first is the conventional kind -
where the bend and stretch of your knees can take you
someplace else
and you feel the wind on your face
knowing that there is a chance
that things are okay,
because that feeling doesn't quite lie in normal domain.
The impossible must be
possible.

Yet,
there is another freedom: a dangerous one.
A forgiving of all transgressions,
a desire in the pit of your stomach
for it would be the most graceful of flights
to heaven
or descent.
There is little left in the outside world that makes sense,
so receding into a dimension that is not this one
seems to be a choice worth thinking on

swinging:
opportunity.
A rare chance, an accident -
tunnel wreckage vision
and a stately funeral regardless.
"Swanning bird swallowed firm"
by asphalt.

Would it be enough?

Graves must be deeper
and justification falls flat -
where must you go now but home?
Can you content yourself
with just swinging?
Crescent moon sky made of nothing -
it can, it could.
Reasonings good
but enough?

Rusted metal chaser down your closing throat…
push it, painless -
but the ground is still there,
your fists are still curled,
asphalt flight postponed:
lack of fuel,
lack of gear,
lack of pilot,
lack of steer.
Lack of everything.
The tear in your vision
is gone.

bedroom

Are you okay?
Yes, with a flick of the hair
And a yoghurt-girl smile.
Up the stairs, shut the door,
And let the muscles sag to floor.
Kick off offending sludge-brown brogues
With nail beds at the collar claw.

Are you sure?
It is gravity, in the throes of passion and lust
Flings us away from the spheres of dust
Beyond the bedroom ceiling
Where idle, the light hangs.
A stiff white neck and a cloying bulb
Flowers down from high above.
As though one could bend around the wire
And look fiercely at the brogues below.

You know I'm always here to talk.
Of what? Of who and what you know?
That was cruel, another stone
Weighs itself down on the bone.
Smile and slap your knee instead
Sit still until your eyes have bled.
Let's swap sandwiches, have some fun
Roll down the hill 'til all is numb.

What's going on with you?
The socks commit fashionable fraud
Found them in the hole in the wall
Put them on the hands at first,

Only shaking for the cold.
Inside, a crater grows, and grows,
Fed by every vicious thought.
A bloody bracelet on arm appears
One that won't erase for years.

Talk to me.
Or we could dance in circles
'Til the body spins in line with head.
Wrap up in the rug once more
A rotting carcass on the floor.
Rainbow underneath the lids
Words lend no colour for this.

Let me hold you.
Hold upright, arms on arms.
Two vultures, feeding on agony.
From the window, from the mirror,
See you in every corner.
Let the tears roll down the pale skin
Like rain in the hollow of a parched leaf.

It's okay. It'll be okay.
Close every day whispering this
Daggers in the sickened flesh.
No-one's there, it's just yourself
Staring back, trying to help.

Blood rises like tide fast
Lapping at the criminal glass
Leaves you covered in sparkling silt

ONCE-JOINED PIECES **65**

Bedroom walls were all you built.

Now like the night with crow's veil
Loneliness hangs upon your sails.
Descend to the ocean bed
With all your ghosts
Scream into the pillow
Swallow more stones
And lay to rest, looking
Down at brogues.

cosm(et)ic procedures

It's an acute angle
that his hand makes, with
his elbow and shoulder
bending so sharp and pointed.
If he did it
it would be obtuse -
the angle,
the pain still acute.
Microdermabrasion
for my tired, imperfect skin
falling away to the crystals of sand
clinging to my feet.
The ocean stretches out:
a silent, glaring bystander
locked in witness protection.
The water cares not for angles and vertexes -
just containment and containers.
Before long it will wash away the footprints,
the sandcastle, forgotten in haste
and caress like a gentle lover
the cliff that contains it,
sift my granules from where they were scattered,
lift them under the moonlight
like a midnight offering,
pull me as I cling to the shore
with futile hopes and misguided freedoms
and release me to the basin of the earth.
Is this where the bereft grains of my soul
will somehow attract back to some certain mass?
How certain is it, really, when sharks and coral and plain
anemone

ONCE-JOINED PIECES **67**

are forgotten here, are hunted here?
In this container there is much to be contained
and no equation to estimate my chances
of ever being found,
of expressing as a whole number.
Must I really let go, to be put back together?
The microderm was irreversible
but perhaps the angles are not.
Reflexes and sand-buckets
to collect fallen treasures -
his hand never meets my cheek
but I lay on that beach
like a fossil from eons before
or perhaps just ten years:
a complex number of once-joined pieces.
I contemplate what is better:
being lost forever
or being broken forever?
Find me, I whisper to the ocean -
found you, water under my feet.

and everything

six-hand phantom limb
cut off from the rest of the building,
one set of double doors
outrunning.
I went to it with nothing
and everything,
and everything.

they heard me sing the same song
a million times,
the sound like a shroud
bearing me out every day
in sombre procession.
exhaustion welled from my eyes
my fingers itched neath the fabric -
it would tear,
I'd run back there:

Lady Gaga wrote Hair
to reclaim,
to awaken from numbness;
so I went and I felt
precious arms prepare me
to find that piece,
piano keys warmer than a home
I could stay in forever.
cotton spooled round my head
and everything drowned out;
everything but that room
touched my tips and buried me too:
me -
I reclaimed.

I was blue

72   ONCE-JOINED PIECES

basin

there is little else
the sound of the pain echoing
in my boundless mind
*

the tears are one with
the water swimming along
wayward like tadpoles
*

they grow into frogs
in the strangest time machine
drowning in the drain

blue

The waves roll into shore at Hawke's bay:
blue, like him. She loves oceans too
with her hat, glasses on,
low cliffs, unstable rock.
Toes bloody climbing up,
staring back at the promise
that was broken.

Conspiration ringing up close for the big show:
sirenic sound. Turn and go,
leave all that is good
behind you.
To the bluest of lies,
she came to.
Her bluest goodbye
for him.

heartbreak on the telephone

How many tears can two eyes hold?
Heartbreak on the telephone.
I wondered when this day would come,
when we'd take this turn around the sun.
Two words and then swift
goodbye into a nether world.
My heart was on a market stall
being bartered with pennies
long before I knew the call,
but it always ended unsold.
It kept ringing
every day but now
I guess I can be sure
every time:
it isn't you.

things I learned when you left

Really, that I was fallible
    that bobble-hats can be haunting
    that the carpet is immensely interesting
    to press your ear against
I learned the meaning of rain
    in rivulets through cobblestones
    that when we throw stones in the ocean
    they go
I learned that there was a muscle behind
    my lungs
    that tugs
    that oxygenated blood
    is still cold, not warm
I learned the meaning of consequence
    the physics of motion
    that it was I
    who had made myself alone
How to live without sending you the
    newest track to dance on
    how to enjoy it on my own
How to be a person
    that would not lean
    like that tower in Pisa
    on air, in between
I learned that forgetting the sound of your voice was
    worse than antidepressants
    grating on my tongue
That soulmates are not soulmates
    if you do not know them
I learned to train my digestive system
    in morsels, in crisps,
    in jam sandwiches
    that there were two kinds of empty

I learned to doodle badly
        rude drawings of my lecturers
        stars on my hands
I learned how to dissociate at bus stops
        that you would not be around the corner
        and I could go under
        pain as if it were anaesthetic
I learned to love rollercoasters
        the feeling of flinging far away
        from ground to sky
        the rush, I could die
How time is a concept so inconsequential
        when minutes are infernal
        and do not go anywhere
I learned to rock on my heels and stand on my tiptoes
        ready to run, seemingly weightless
        like you were to me
I learned to take down the photos
        your face must be different now
        your hair could be brown, or red, or blue
        that I will always hold the memory of you
How my threads could unravel
        a spinster to spin for eons
        to create a person again
        that can learn
perfectly well,
I count my self-diminishing traits
        before I calculate friendships
        and skirt the line of love and sickness
Learnings when you left
        were tall and mighty and chest-bearing

I only wear one pair of shoes
and perhaps that was it
But when you left, my heart fused with carpet-fibres
and my nose to the ground
I thought only about the sound
of your laugh
my feet on the armchair next to yours
our notes and our math
how your ears must have been warm
under that bobble hat.

brushing

The bristles – there must be hundreds of them
screeching against enamel
foaming from left to right.
Every movement
requires the strength of ten thousand lions
the patience of a million tiny black ants.
Near impossible for thoughts to avoid black holes
and reflections in mirrors
red mixing with white
eyes sticking on eyes.
In the fraction of a second
it takes for the brain to tell the arm
to tell the hand to tell the fingers
to curl and pull
push and repeat
my will is shattered.
Let them rot, I think.
It would be better than having to brush.

dive

I am trying to breathe

The world does not shake as it extricates
the air from me -
as if it were so easy;
as if it were the hiss of a balloon that slipped between my
fingers
out into the nether.

I am trying to breathe -
fill the lungs,
feel the diaphragm shift
the parts, the essence
maybe I'm missing
what humans do
for humans -
are supposed to breathe.

Hold it - two, three and
out, two, three and
in
to the fearful place,
the racing heart,
the crushing weight
and let it go, two, three -
it's getting old, two three -
and knowing God high above
can see
I am trying to breathe.

Press my face into the water,

slow, slow
down we go,
trick my mind
in some faraway archipelago,
down, down
into the dark
slow, slow waves
slow, slow shades
of blue, and glass, and white
behind my eyes,
I am trying not to breathe.

Left to right,
rock the boat,
see what happens if
you topple and float,
cool as ice
it rains in space
more than it does here
you see,
it is safe
where no-one has to breathe,
to live,
for no-one lives.

There is a light at the corner of my vision
blinking through the dark,
my scopes don't know stars
from black holes
and for sailors in the dead of night,
both of them burn.

I don't want to breathe.

The waves foam,
the dreams go,
the boat fills
and I don't know if it is
the trap that I ensnared myself in long ago -
oh too, that serendipity of dwindling oxygen
or even the tragedies that I could never quite dissect
or separate from my soul.
Some days I fancy it as depression -
I do not fault the name
but how does this creature
know mine?

I cannot hope,
I cannot plan,
I cannot think of life as more than
the starfish in my throat
when I wake
once again.

I don't want to breathe
for breath belongs
to someone else
someplace else;
breath belongs to those who can cherish,
it belongs to those who dedicate,
who navigate
waterways
like this.

Give me the oars then.
Give me the wood.
Give me the people
and perhaps I should
build, like Nuh did:
construct a sail,
a muscle
to rail
against the shock of cartilage
and lift
and give
and feed
and live
and rest, perhaps
in the absence of gravity,
in and out
side to side
slow
slow
down you go
into the dark
into the pain
and toss up the rigging
and there we stay,
brimming in God's infinite basin,
just underneath,
moment by moment -
I am trying to breathe.

deadfoot

I'm betrayed by the glass
crunching underfoot
roughed up on grass
no ceremony to boot
closest I've ever been
to watching my own demise
could well be my organs
flayed out in disguise
mine would be more a mess
less invisible, less danger
mine would be sorry that
you let your gaze wander
you can't stretch flesh back together
limbs don't reattach
hearts don't start again
and they certainly don't whisper
when you step on them
they don't penetrate
unless you linger
but then you'd see
they were broken long before they were broken
and you can't fix something broken
when it died that way.
Screw it, it's a funeral
Not mine
We'll die to see another day.

say something

I.
eager eyes
cheeks stretching bare
tentative smile
hands clasped in prayer

eyes peeled
nervous stare
jittering knee
throat aching for air

eyes red
stomach clawed in
jilting mind
wearing thin

II.
Do they whisper?
Do they tilt their head
with pity?
Do they start conversations
or do they end them?
Do they want me to go
or do they want me to join them?
What can I do to not be a burden -
do they want me
or not?

III.

to go or not to go
to reply or to ignore
I want no questions asked
I want to hide
I want to laugh
I want a sign
I want doors shut
I want to end the pain
I want to scream so loud
they'll all stay away.
The confusion is deafening
as the thump of my heart
in earnest to find
where I will rest.

IV.

Maybe this is how it's supposed to be:
heart somersaulting as I answer the phone,
too scared to tell the man my order is wrong,
going to the toilet for two minutes of calm,
mustering the strength to go out, carry on,
cartwheeling, jump-jacking performance
to be funny, to be notorious,
wanting to be visible but hating the spotlight,
crying after meet-ups in measure of my plight,
not eating in front of you - I'll definitely spill it,
skin flaming, nausea sitting
deep as the despair in my bones,
leaping out of my way in the way of good books,
despising the waste of the space that I took.

When someone asks if you're alright, I just smile and mean it.
The answer is never what they want
and I'm afraid to not mask it.
In truth, every second,
the freedom of my mind crushes
against the weighted planes of my knotted chest.
It cannot greet the world everyday -
but the world everyday
urges me, a mouse on a string,
do it: say something.

V.
say something
say something
say something
God, just say it

you useless idiot.

haunt me subtly

Do I dream of you so often
because my body is trying to forget you?
You visit me with such regularity
yet the pain never lessens.
I may put to bed the guilt and the shame
but I cannot seem to leave your face in the attic
of my brain.
You seep through me like floodwater
salting every door.
I cannot remember your voice, or really your features
but the picture remains
like a ghoul hanging beside me as I war with sleep.
You are never to be severed
and I am not sure I want you to be,
but you could have some consideration
and pack yourself into a corner,
tape yourself into a box.
I guess I always knew you were a free spirit
even your memory cannot be caged,
but oh, little bird, release me.
Haunt me, but do it with subtlety.

once-joined pieces

Can you be broken if you were already broken?
There must be a limit -
a finite number of pieces
your heart can collapse to.
The end? No, it never comes,
even by choice.
There are no yellow page numbers
when you are breaking
at logarithmic rates,
with steep multiplicity.
There is just a continuous line
and there is no coming back.
What they took from me -
what I took from me -
it's never coming back.
I eat, but I'm still empty,
I smile, but warmth feels lengthy
when cold?
Cold is my companion.
Me and my continuous line,
trying, and just trying
somehow to make it back
to a beginning.

But my once-joined pieces
do not accompany
and the little girl inside of me
will never forgive
what I did
and what I could never
rebuild. She sits like

my jury on my chest
and pathetically,
I present my case:
I was broken, and I am broken today.
What she put in my hands
slipped through like rice grains,
for there are holes
and there are whole
ambitions that she burdened me with.
So I apologise, your honour
for my extortionate rates,
I have tried, and I will try again.
But she should, in all fairness
cease wanting inflexion -
I am a crash course in pre-morbid direction.
She should learn,
She should cave,
She should adjudge me some peace
and she should save
the inquisition for my heart
that was breaking
all that time ago
two halves on the floor.
Dole out her sentence
for the original sin,
forgive my once-joined pieces
we weren't destined to win.

it would be easier if I knew I didn't matter

so well, and if I didn't know
this business,
this sordid business
of deciding what comes next

my kite-tails preen for long-distance
second star to the right and
no resistance
none that matters

wind is air after all -
but heavy in my chest,
unsuitable for Icarus wings
just aching for melting doom.

fly on, fly free
why on? why free?
bounds in the boundless
everywhere I see

the rightness of cutting Fate's string;
a sky of wax and feathers -
but up there Daedalus watches always
the edges of the sun.

dry

dry
my throat is dry
my eyes are dry
my hands are dry
my skin
so often a bed of rivers
baked silent like a desert
even the pain is parched
dry lips stick together
as dry mind wavers
is it advantageous to rain?
but in the passenger seat
on a mission to kill
I am dry
for my nothing
is what keeps them away.

destroy me

I lay down my towers so easily
when there is someone who could hurt me.
I can taste pain with my index up in the wind
and I let the conquerors wade through willingly.
Impenetrably penetrable by the right words
and the right voices,
I let blunt knives strike at old wounds
as if I long for the sight of my own blood,
my head on a harpoon.
Welcome invasion, stone-slat skin raising its pores
to open, latching
on to every arrow curling in;
let it raze me to the ground,
burning each turret as it falls,
smoking columns, crumbling walls -
let it ruin, leave nothing standing,
I hold my white flag miles away:
tell them, destroy me, you can stay,
plunder and pillage to your heart's content.
Take it all, take more:
parapets and floors.
Just make sure,
make haste,
no grey,
no trace.
Keep going -
I want nothing left.

Dadiamma

I remember the gully where my grandma lived
I remember peering, out through her curtains
at the passers-by,
sniffing the petrol in my uncle's motorbike
Karachi's air at night was so markedly different
it smelt like life
eager and moving
the wind coming in from the distant ocean
I remember the steps up on to the roof
and how I hated that the door was locked
I remember the room
where we would line up our suitcases
the cupboard in which she kept
her meagre purchases
I remember her standing at the hob
boiling milk, her russet hands
shaking at the job
She had photos of her children
and her children's children
tacked up where she slept
I remember her crumpled smile
and the way she wept
when she prayed to her maker
her late-night secrets
how easy I could wake her
I remember how she held my head in her lap
put her knitting needles aside
when I cried back in England
she'd stroke my hair to the side
I remember thinking that at least she cared
in my hothead teenage days

that when I sunk into the sofa
in an ashen daze
that she would sit up, kind eyes
and I never gave
it thought
I saw only how I was alone
but when she chided gently
as I read books in the dark
I remember she noticed.

Later, when she was gone
I remember we found her letters
her diploma
the lives she gave up
to buy pens
to cook dinner
all for her granddaughter
to wear out notebooks
to forget what she taught her
I remember the way she used to draw the rose
and how I showed it off
that she would draw pictures for me to paint
that her world was about building
and sketching
pinning and sewing
always knowing,
how four walls were enough
and how giving mattered only
when it was giving for love
I remember the moment I returned to the gully
stepped over the threshold that would never forget her

and it felt the same, in my bedroom in Gloucester
as I saw the bed that had also lost her
her comb in my drawer
her biscuits uneaten
but what she left, far more
that night at her door
sent by their mothers
who trusted no other
they came in their hundreds
her students of colour.

chronicity

when something bad happens to you -
for the first length of time, you internalise it
pack it away
maybe even forget
leave it buried at the bottom of your mind
under a cotton-wool blanket
put to bed the feeling.

days, months, years
of skimming stones
one day comes the remembering
crushing your bones
the reliving
the fainting on sink edges
the curl of air
invading
up your nostrils
the poison in everything.

after that, the breaking
the admitting, often at gunpoint
the spoken and the truth
the distant dark corners of your vision
someone else breaks through

imperiously, there comes the reckoning
the recognising that the red hands
do not belong to you
it is not your fault
it wasn't you
for moments you believe it too

for a time you say the same things
you wear shades of self-acceptance

but then comes realisation
that loving yourself harder than
what happened to you
is like resuscitation
on a corpse
only ten times worse
for you can save others
with your folding heart
but for yourself it doesn't start

then, as it happens,
you grieve
you mourn for your soul
spliced even and integrated
you sit in dead grass fields
burning for words
as the sun siphons the sky away
and your pain is there to stay
you wonder what you did
know you didn't do anything
in this space, you melt heavy
onto the hay
blinking back cars and red capsules
you fill the stupid fridge
laden on the mix
you grieve minute
by each minute.

when something bad happens to you
it lives there in your skin
as night penetrates evening
the clothes you wear are thin
despite layers and grass you have grown
thin enough to feel the cold.

100   ONCE-JOINED PIECES

I was fish

102   ONCE-JOINED PIECES

trying

my feet at the edge
I contemplated options
and chose fear again
*

what we had, I shout
from rooftops but you can't hear
how I drowned for you
*

my eyes kept closing
when the morning came
and my line was still empty

hope is

every inch of you.
Every memory, every experience,
every moment you have suffered,
every mountain you have climbed
and every birth in the gutter:
every synapse.
Every particle of your being
tells you there is not nothing

waiting

I am waiting;
waiting like a snake.
Cool and raw this side of the moon,
I have shed my skin
and now I wait.

Bag of flesh and bones, weary,
still fury in the undergrowth.
Treading where the sun is a stranger,
I wait with eyes open, in thrall,
I must be alert, I must see all.

Broke-backed blue-blooded disparity;
there they are at the top
and here I am on the floor.
What, for carrying a thousand mes, selves,
shelled, cold-cracked, shellacked in my woes?

Not one of them can climb to the boughs,
not one of them can find home amidst
the soil. The festering sequelae of departed souls
pulls and pulls hard; I hide in the brown
skin, hoping that they will mistake me.

The ground is a sea: a sea of skin
and each day I swim, harder, hoping
the tide will rise when I grow one that can win.
Waiting for that unfolding sky.
Under the trees and over the grim -

strong enough, tough enough, enough enough;

I am impatient, I cast off another.
Eyes passed down in reptile millennia
to watch, to fail, to fail, to wait:
wear my skins, watch my fate.

what do my eyes look like behind the lids?

no-one's ever bothered to know. or find out
whether they're still brown,
or still round,
still filled,
still sound
after the cracks at first glance.
no-one wonders how my pupils dance
from graphic to nothing,
from upstairs floor-casting
to downstairs star-gazing,
leftmost extreme
to right-handed dream,
devastating eyelet beams
into caricatures of life.
no-one thinks about the price
my eyes pay for every moment of dark,
possession of calm
a commodity charmed
in existence, washing in absence,
they bathe in moments.
no-one knows they are precious,
not even I
shattered windows
and window shutters
hide scars still invisible inside.
no-one questions what my eyes look like
behind the lids,
because perhaps they know
at least one thing
that I don't
and sorely wish I could:

when I am gone, as costly as it proves
and as delicious the numb,
that I am still here in front of them.

my sorry bed

counting to three
holds such a curious power:
mystically destined, or else ill-fated,
a delirium, baited breath as the words
leave your lips
as if the dying notes of a number three
are Israfil's trumpet
and you would be sorry.
so I count, naturally,
and threaten myself with oblivion,
that self-same friend.
listen out for
the trill, the whistle, the magic
I rouse my sincerities
to ambition, to life and to all I hold dear,
ready, able -

and one:
traverse this land, make it your own
make it so others will know a home
need is aplenty, your hands are warm
do not give up in the eye of the storm
your world is out there, if you let it in
wear what was done right on your chin.
I meet my world every day, I promise you
there is only so much that
one can do
my chin is tired
my legs won't move
but still, somehow, there is scope

for two:
shoes are out, dress is pressed
you go out looking your best
bargaining time, a prize for the fight
a dog and its bone in the morning light
close your eyes and picture the breath
you will breathe as you conquer death
you win and here is your warranty
fight, there's no time it's almost -
oh bed, oh safe bed, here comes

three:
oh bed where for a time I am free
the trumpet is my background noise
my childhood friend, forever poised
to soothe me with its final tone
warm bed, safe bed - I won't go

oblivion cannot scare me
a fool's errand entirely
count I do
I count to three
but the Angel of Death comes not for me
writhe in wait
for some blinding light
whatever will end this endless night

once more
I count
make it to three?
on my feet, high tide
river into the sea

110   ONCE-JOINED PIECES

my best laid plans, my tearing hopes
count again
three steps
climb cliffs and slopes
count again
The Angel will wait for his divine call
one, two, three
don your coat
one, two, three
wear your chin
open that door
open sky
just out of reach
she's rare, that grey
but so are each
to their own
and I set my store

count again,
magic words
my sorry bed will miss me so
this wretched dance
for just one tomorrow
for the benefit of some
still God will make the end
an unexpected one.
count again
count again
until I can count no more
and bloodied and bruised
I am out of the door.

hoarder

the room untarnished by ruin
evades me.
handles in the corridor tried and tested,
found and harvested
for more.
if I find it -
I fill it.
I fill it with doubt, dread,
all manner of hoarding
and then I close the door,
mark it with red paint,
it'll do for a rainy day.
Each empty space I find is the one:
the one that will be different.
White walls and bright windows,
trellised with tulips,
rosewood floor…
and as I tear down the walls,
rip the heads off the flowers,
hammer through the floor -
I evade the chance
of what it could have been
and what it will now forever be:
ruined.

forgetting, for some time

On my bus seat -
the number five to the station,
I'm pondering food
and debating existence,
for am I really here, in my head,
in this bus?
Did the driver see me when I got on?
Would it matter if I just
sailed round and round the route all day
with my £4.50 day pass?
It would certainly pay
to be somewhere where existence
is not a conundrum.
Where being here means being there
and making the most of
moments, I am tired.
Eyes smarting
try to listen to thrumming bass,
glancing out at darkening skies,
the dipper on the headlights;
Be bold, do something,
do something please -
we must slip underneath.
Pour your water down the aisle
and swim out to sea
to lands where no-one knows your name
Where you're still you
but not the same
Where shoes fit your Cinderella feet
dancing in sandy ballrooms,
no station platforms,

we'd wedge-heel, inevitable contusions
down the strait,
aisle-seats on their toes,
throwing petals and peddling
polaroid smiles,
needling the living and my God it
beguiles.
I fancy that I am there
not here
and who is the cosmos to argue
when in dazzling disarray
its passengers clamber
to forgetting, for some time.
Stops are irrelevant
when you ride for spots
across your eyes,
as you stare at the light too long,
blinkers, sleepers, chatters
and non-existers
Swings and roundabouts,
this forgetting,
and the person in the adjacent seat:
workplace drama and deceit
has not yet mastered
or perhaps not aware
of what we do here,
but they will learn.
As did I, on the number five
and I learned it well
enough to lose the key
down the drain

the moment I'd pay
for this precious commodity.
Slip in, wash away
with tulip rain
in one discerning piece -
hungry, but not for food,
Four-fifty for forgetting
and nock back my earnings;
I ate
for a thousand this morning.

remembering

Three seconds before
I'd forgotten,
I imagined ice,
bedding my brain.
I knew freezing was possible -
I remembered that fear doesn't last forever.
I can build the world that I wanted to.

But like water buoying droplets of oil,
my blood silt-lifts what cannot mix
to the surface.
I know that I must
siphon it,
raze it,
let the feelings go -
they cannot hold me anymore.
I have to do it now
as they swim like tadpoles up for air;
I must not let them breathe.
I must not bury another world
before it has yet to still grow legs.
I must brave it.

But what they told me isn't true;
these moments aren't there to be braved.
Swans everywhere are ugly
and they were born that way.
Trauma sits in me
to watch me play:
play at three-second pauses,
play at peace,

play at Person,
only to show its face
in the aisle of the train
as I'm moving,
to teach me for my game at braving.
It crazes,
erases
reasons for living through anything that lasts as long
or as short-lived as worlds, oh you know

I'd stumble, holding ice to its face.
If I never knew that it would never end,
I would be brave.
But for all I remember about fear,
I just go on
f*cking
remembering.

show me the sky

My sunflower stalk
grows out at the back of the garden
Alone.
Relies on the heavens for rain
and despite our ways
some form of shooting stem
crept from the untilled soil,
brown and thin
like a snake's coil,
pith crusting away.
It sprouted under a bed of weeds
that stunted its growth:
Long, not tall
and there in the dirt, it saw seasons -
the birds flew south for the winter,
the squirrels with their nuts, preparing for hibernation.
Head on its side, it watched as the snowdrops came,
and then the bluebells
tipped in lilac and dressed in dewy silk,
faring for a moon at most
before they too fed the earth
and there it lay, half-alive,
for though they burned bright
they knew the sky,
grew intimate with bumblebees,
entertained butterflies
and rattled in the wind -
precarious living.

We forgot that we planted it there
and if we remembered,

then what?
Tape marks and string, scarecrow on a cross?
Blooming on one's deathbed
is rather a subcutaneous end;
petals to ashes in one fell swoop,
dinner for the critters.
It is not there yet, but I will be,
and here and now, embittered in our ways:
sunflowers were meant to reach for the sun
and I have not yet seen the sky.

guilt

you must make them monsters
to assuage your guilt,
crushing under your tongue
lozenge for the wicked,
trading in their families
for uncertain returns:
investment, startup costs
beyond your stupid ideals of right and wrong.
Do it for the rush:
the burn when you feel right and alright for two seconds,
offering up shattered promises
like a glimmering oath to boundless infinities
between the joy and the hurt.
Make it further and further:
a turtle's daughter, hatched on the sand up high,
writhing forth to black tide
where her siblings await and where she cannot hide
from storms and predators,
from loss and lots that is better.
Death for the thousandth time when you touch the shore
and when it washes you over and you crave for more:
remember the firmness of sand between your toes
and the darling you have forsworn
for nothing, and everything
flashes when you have nothing -
do it, again
they are monsters,
you are swimming.

waiting room

Do I wish someone was here, holding my hand?
I don't know.
I don't know if what's missing is someone else,
or if it's me, vacant from my frame.

22 minutes past,
spirits dance through paintings.
Drown in Ophelia's lake,
brushes of Victorian absurdity,
swaddled in splendorous vice,
holding apples and looking dutiful
or waving goodbye to war bound boy-men
with spotted handkerchiefs and made-up jazz ensembles,
fringey dresses or lounging on chaises…

no, I'll sail the watercolour sea my friend painted -
the first time I knew the colour blue
and fell in love irrevocably.
Better, in my year 6 topic book Morpurgo river;
I didn't know loss then,
I painted with blue but it was just blue,
then,
I made pink impressions on bitten fingernails,
disappeared into the picture book
ink blot holographic pages
but now the waiting room walls
have little in the way of escape;
they'll weigh me on the scale
whilst I think of the whale
from Sinbad, and how it slept
and how I wish too to sleep

ONCE-JOINED PIECES 121

long enough for life to grow.

Render my emptiness in every bloody painting,
dip every brush into the pot and whatever I remember
will spill out,
for the entire gallery to see.
But no-one will dance,
no-one will sit and disappear into me.
Plaster cast any shoes that will fit:
make them ruby and just make me live.
Leave empty canvases,
what's to say after this?
The doctor will tell me 'just see how it is'.

I have to let him down

The feeling knots my insides
like a boa with the death squeeze.
Letting people down has never ended well.
I must not let anyone down.
But I have to, today.
He is ten minutes away -
and I am ten years away
from when I first knew I was missing,
still yet finding footholds
on a mountain of mist
expected to summit and plant a flag
where nothing but I exist.

Entertain the notion that abandonment is not my best suit
but God, this is all I have been doing
since the moment I stood outside the head's office:
head bowed in shame, head made of flame
It was then that I learned to leave me
leave me to my subconscious devices
leave others to their humanly emotions
I have to let him down
and boa-squeeze a heart that falsely claims to be
just like his.
I am ten seconds from freefall
ten steps from a bridge
ten thousand reasons why
it is better I am missed.

fish on a line

To forget the lines on your face –
nightmare shapes
will never fade.

All the stars –
you were supposed to point them out.
Now I'm filled with doubt
that they're there at all.

Fish on your line,
I bent to all your whims –
oh, I crumbled
at your fingertips.

Call it love –
maybe it was once.
Like the sun,
everything finds its end.

Empty hopes, promises, pain
and hurt.
In your hands
I am bone and dust.

Fish on your line,
I bent to all your whims –
push me out to shore
and I'll keep looking

for what you took
and what I gave.

Just think -

when I find
the stars,
you'll be staring
at the dark -
fish on a line.

Wind will change,
I'll swim away.

grief

at the bus stop, sweat drips down my back
I was late before I left
same pale blue sky
a different me to yesterday
still, it's you I think about
as the world races past.

ONCE-JOINED PIECES 127

128 ONCE-JOINED PIECES

I am boat

130   ONCE-JOINED PIECES

onward

froth licks up my sides,
a wash of greeting. I don't
know if I should say goodbye
*

outgrowing the shell
I still search for the pieces
to build the new one
*

I am boat. I set
out in the dark with no-one
and my wishing stone

blank spaces

The invites to my wedding have
not yet been sent out.
I have not yet decided on a date,
I have not designed the menu
and I have not designed a husband.
Just i's to dot,
t's to cross;
blank spaces I'll jot
down answers to
but you

are not a blank space.
You will not be at my wedding,
but I will not miss you,
because you won't have a spot
that I stare at, way across

the classroom; I won't wait
for you outside
with a lily bouquet
or a crisis,
I will not have anything for you.

My coal blue armchair,
my first-year bedroom -
will not be missed,
and as one that knows absence,
I am sure of this.
I will not rip up name cards,
sob and scream in my dress;
you will not be something

I have need to forget

for I will not have your voice
and I will not hear your breaths,
you will not haunt the space that you left.

You will still matter, and you always will
but my body will not twist
at your name,
wish you had stayed -
I will realise,
and I know I will:
I do not have to.

horizon

Slow riding in wheat-fields,
plumes of gold perfuming the air
for butterflies to dance a commotion -
dragging skin, red-raw skin
stretching, etching
impressionist strokes,
light changes
pasts upon palms
but the horizon hides
beneath a cobalt sky.
Wind whittles a path through
and passes like a breath from your lungs:
once yours, now gone
to someplace else,
laughter dying in its burst
trailing and echoing in silent cacophony.
Home is that way.
But riding west, away from the sun,
the corners are violet
and maps run out,
no directions left
to cut paths.
Hands empty - dance the dance
dear one,
dance the commotion
'til the tomorrow dawn comes.

I'm not sorry I married the wind

I'm not sorry I married the wind -
for you weren't there
and were never going to be.
I would've had you if you wanted me.
But now, no -
I am not sorry.
The wind I can hold,
with wind I am held,
the way I thought I was with you.
I'm not sorry for keeping promises
because I mean them -
and I kept mine to you.
I reached out, and
I married the wind.

swim

for Polly

Not a single part of me accepts that it's over -
there is so much more I wanted to wade into with her,
a tale as swashbuckling as the Princess Bride;
that impossible swamp they escape into.
It's a classic, you know:
sensations with endings.
But I have a lot to say -
I don't think I'll ever stop having a lot to say.
Each feeling I try on like a cloak and each one fits;
each Cinderella shoe belongs to me
and I want to wear them
and share them
and trudge all over the world
so that people will hear me
one day,
and I won't get lost in the summer of 2011
ever again
ever again.

Tolerate confusion, let it settle, acknowledge it
but it's a miasma -
it tugs me on the shoulder like an incessant child.
It wants an answer
but offers no hand
out of my Zoo of Death;
level 100, I'm a fish on the line
but she let out the wire
so far I have to fight
the current
and I have to swim away
and somehow I think
she meant for it this way.

Bournemouth

my secret footsteps on Bournemouth beach
on a mild day in July
are the stories I've been burning to tell
giving every goosebump to the water
for I can breathe
here
in between land and ocean
my boots are filling
but my feet are pressing
to jump
and jump hard
let the stories be told.

recompense

I give them hardship
in adversities plenty
Never-ending sagas of
processing gently;
I give them choices
and they choose them
Rivers return
and dance into oceans;
I give them insecurities
not healed by their hand
but worked through carefully
with careful plans;
I give them growth
from moon-eyes to volcanoes
In what they do, who they are
and they have foundations;
I give them person:
albeit flawed,
with intentions that are good
not masked with fraud;
I give them vocation
that livens their souls
A second love
mediates the first's thralls;
I give them a house
that becomes their home
of seedling shoots
and all that they own;
I give them family,
not blood but more
That see them truly,

not parts of wholes;
I give them arguments
because they are human too
in their own way but I admit
it is superficial;
I give them emotions
charged electric, AAs
Love and will win out
and he always stays;
Most of all I give them joy
in abiding for each other
For on their green earth
they were meant to be together;
I give them what I know now as recompense
In some world they exist
Organs of me
Ceased and desist.

They do not have the holes you had patched up
They have tears, accidental ones
Mended, not burned
Their hearts converse
Do not shrivel and curl
Their hearts converse
no matter what befalls.
Their child that I give them
is their colourful world
A symbol of love
into another grows.
They have mishaps
but for it they work

ONCE-JOINED PIECES 139

They do not point fingers
at their four-year-old flying
fish causing all their troubles.
I have them tell him stories
Show him stars
Tell him they once lived
and remind us of it.
I fancy that when their teenage boy
phones home from school
they would employ
some thought and empathy
That when he tells them he wants more than football
they do not rejoice but hear his call
and listen for what they might have missed
They know a mistake for what it is
They take the shots
I give them tough ones
But they sail through tests
Smoking guns
so easy they were to see
if one was looking properly
But they see and hear and do
adoringly.
All that I want I give them
for I have no-one to receive
No-one I want
and will ever
For they are it all
All you were never
And less I will not give
on to another.

140 ONCE-JOINED PIECES

sister
for Jia

I wish I had known
you before I decided
I was made alone.

There is me and you
and the rest of the world – one
day I'll understand

my heart can be safe
and for yours I'll go to war -
you are everything.

the robin

the robin lives for average only a year and a bit
susceptible to cold weather and territorial digs
so curious, it seems, when he ignores the risks
and tattoos a robin on the cusp of his ribs.

everyone said it, even she
she'd never live to thirty-three
one arrow and she'd be gone
and to tell the truth he did fear loss -

uncanny how life persists
despite the very worst of it
he'll die with that bird on his skin
against all odds, outliving.

Billie

How terrifyingly possible
for a name to heal?
We found many a name in
those art-crust backstreets -
where I watched you grow up
and you taught me that love
can be fiercer than the love
I traded in.

Your name rang bells,
found the seat next to mine -
scribbled in the ruled lines of my heart,
running deep across the margins.
I heard you before I saw you;
I knew you were there,
and I knew your light would not dim.
You were purple and determined
to make it all a part of your journey -
catching moments like racing leaves in autumn wind,
holding them up to me and telling me:
breathe them in.

I watched you fly and I wept when I could not,
when your wings faltered too -
I did not know how to hold you.
It was all I had on the tip of my tongue -
the weight of what we had done
together to survive.

You chose still to be all that you had said you would
back when we asked each other the big questions.

ONCE-JOINED PIECES 143

I watched you take on your true name
and let it become the root of all that was yet to grow -
there was never a time you lifted your eyes to mine
that I didn't know
what it took to tend that garden.
In fresh-turned soil on your hands and knees -
you showed me each seedling
and each blooming shrub,
pointing adamantly to the prettiest one,
saying 'look, that's you, you're growing here too'.

Your name, my friend
is that place you birthed and bred
in the backstreets, in the airports,
in the five-point buildings that crumbled around you -
that place where you let me find you
and you found it all in me.
That place we never thought we would get to
but sang of and fought to -
you made it possible.
The place where we learned
we could love again.

tilted heads

in the dream, the two pieces fit
like footfalls into a beat,
and there were colours
like I had never seen.

she'll be Joan, he said
and he can be Didion;
it's like we were writing with the same pen.

I remember feeling eyes on me -
not scrutinising…just eyes.
his treehouse looked over my courtyard
and we gazed…
he had dark eyes, I know,
and the kind of tall
that crests dark moons
out of reach.

I still feel the way that behind their backs
on the balcony,
we witnessed the night
and he tilted his head to the right
so it just touched mine
and he didn't pull back.
purple smoke in the air and
my skin, his hair
a brush of the thumb;
for that second, beyond my world,
I knew something that I do not know.

when I wore the clothes he sent

ONCE-JOINED PIECES 145

streams down my arms and legs
every word like current in water
'doesn't red look good on her?'
in my fortress, I was
his words on willow-paper.

but just before I realised,
I remembered my smile;
I hadn't written his Didion -
I didn't trust him yet,
but in that midnight sky,
my eyes wept red
for my soul, I saw stars
that were not yet dead.

imperfect women

Strong and brave, they'd call us.
Strong, brave, broken;
Strong, damaged women -
battered and bruised.

Strong and brave
for What We've Been Through:
flattened tarmac
shiny and new
like the hamster wheel,
turning again in search of food.

Strong and brave down the avenue,
plastered into one piece,
arms linked,
sailing through, they see us
broken and bruised,
and they love our
depression bed 'can do'.

We look at each others' faces
and not a word is said.
We know that line under our eyes
the same way our nail beds
know blood-tired
tearing women:
neglect to neglected,
rejecting, rejected.
Brave gets us there,
strong lifted heads,
but there is only road

and more road
we must lay yet.

Strong and brave hopeless women,
waiting for what we never really get;
enough means nothing
and nothing is enough,
atrophied arms holding up
hearts that cared too much
and watched it cost us,
keying change out of our pockets
for the three minutes of calm.
'Notice the air in your lungs
how alive you've become'.

Strong and brave un-dead women,
tombstone circle and quiet incantations,
rest in the dark;
we're here to work
but we want to sleep
under our blanket of soil.
We look at our feet,
battered and bruised on the sun-scorched road,
tears streaming soft
and there it is:
the oasis.
We connect;
we're connected
in skeins, skin
sails sewn at the water's edge.

148 ONCE-JOINED PIECES

Strong and brave imperfect women,
striving for perfection
but finding each other:
five jacks on a beanstalk,
five fingers on a hand
clenching on the mast
as we shake on our land.
All our bloody trap doors lie open,
no more road to surface -
dolphins burst
in sparkling traces,
high and tall…
With one hand each we grab hold,
soar into the unknown
eyewall
as the hurricane of strong and brave rises around us.
We hold tight,
and look at one another.
Fear is true,
scars stay forever,
still;
we're on this boat
together.

you

I can see you

> Yes,

you.

> Little lost one.

Yes, it's true that you're far away

> but so am I

> and I can see

> > you.

She cast me out, but she forgot
I wouldn't go far.

> Just as you, I made my shell
> on the edge -

> > slow

invisible   silver   streak.

My sight sharpened, across light years
of forgotten love

> and I saw

> > you

> streak past

                                        little lost star.

We are slaves to gravity,
yet the universe expands
moment   upon   moment.

The shell will feel snug,
I promise that   home   is   home   one day.

Here in your orbit, ahead of your time -
          I am the edge, I know there will be more

and every shell in the whole wide world
                    will be little, lost and yours.

bungalow

I want
a bungalow.
I tell everybody I want a park-view apartment
but really,
I want a bungalow.

I want tulips in the spring,
bluebells and heather
wisteria and a pond
for water-lilies and fishes.
I want a path paved in
with grass thick trim
to lead up to an ochre door
raised on a white-wood porch
housing hanging baskets and wellies.

I want, to be honest,
a Volkswagen Beetle
powder-blue, four-seater
and a gorgeous bike
inside a side-gate
and for weekends,
roller-skates,
though we'd have to drive
to the skate park for that
make fools of ourselves
and then arm-in-arm to
the independent cafe
where you and I
love to hate
the smell of pumpkin
but we love the hot chocolate.

We will buzz home
and in our green kitchen
you'll get started on dinner
whilst I whip together
some sugary confection
that you will despise me for
but will always give in.
once I am done,
I will help as I'm able
God, I want
a great big turntable
with my records on a shelf
and I'll play them as we dance
on potato skins
if your shoulders get weary
I'll pause, and lean in
and say nothing
but wrap my arm round you
lay my head as you stir
you will know I am there
you will know I am yours.

I want a dining room, sure
but I want a smaller table
in that kitchen
for just us
so I can cross my legs,
tie up my hair and do a happy
lasagne-dance
and you will laugh at me.

I want a room,
we'll call it 'my study'
but the walls will be papered by
my posters and buddies
I'll have mood lighting,
sheer purple drapes
moon-tapestries
and candles
Under the south-facing window
I want a digital piano
I want lessons on how to read
the music that I love
I want my ukulele collection to have its own display
and of course, one wall
will be books and books and books
and I want to read them.
I will have a desk, for work reasons
but I want a loveseat in one of the corners
a tiny tall table with a tassel-lamp
to curl up next to
with my notebook
or instrument
or latest new novel
You'll come and fetch me if I
fall asleep
shake your head and grumble
your office will be far more fit to purpose
I want you to have your space
and make it your own.

I want a bedroom, simple beauty
a four-poster, oak furniture

a dressing table, a big mirror
walk-in wardrobe, his and hers
You'll always snap under your breath
throw out the odd curse
at my messy orders
But will relent when I remind you
you can't see the clutter.
Slippers on a corner-rug
White curtains made of sheer damask
I want my favourite stupid photo of us
on my bedside table.

I want a cherry-blossom tree outside our window
I want you to hold my hand
I want shorter hair
and I want lash extensions
I want laser treatment
and a body that listens
I want you to love my friends as I love them
and for lunches together
a place to stay, if ever they need
you will know that they were my oxygen
when I couldn't breathe.
I want a cupboard just for mugs
and I want to do something arty
with my postcards
I want city-breaks
and to be whisked away
a backpack and my Polaroid
to see beautiful places
and do beautiful things

ONCE-JOINED PIECES 155

to look at you and feel
as if I have wings
I want sunglasses that fit
I want to be hip
I want ridiculous earrings and
for you to enable

I want to run hands through hair
and never to feel
afraid of abandon
or being myself
I want family
with whom I am stable
with whom you manage
to break bread, tell tales
I want to go to concerts and
sit on your shoulders
I want to try glitter
and have you laugh when it fails
but touch my cheek with your fingers
and give me those eyes
time to go home otherwise
I'll cry ugly tears when it's over
and you know me too well, it's familiar

I want you to know me
and still want me.
I want to know you
and not wonder.

Oh, hell, I want walks by a river
I want conversations

that go hither and thither
I want to sing
and I want you to listen
I want you to be proud
of my every admission
I want to work at walking distance
with children who are unaware that
their existence is a miracle
that I was them, and they will be me
I will be patient,
I will build foundations
I want what I do to make a difference
To see them unfold
and sew together
their world - our world.
I want to be great, I want kids
to be kids
not mine,
just living,
I want to understand
having my own
and for you to wait
until I am ready
I want to be a three, maybe
The bungalow will hold
and I want us to be better
for it.

I want my tears to have purpose
to never be futile
I want the moments

I want the comfort
of not needing to say words
of just being, existing
with you, not alone.
I want you to be the object of my words
I want to show you this poem
and evidence my claims
that I in fact, dreamed you up
we are imperfect together
I want a good forever.
I want ice-cream, a garden, to meet heroes
to write songs, to have baths, to indulge
I want money, I will be careful
for I know what I have given
to make this my home
and believe in it.

I want the park-view apartment only
if it is
I, and I alone.
But, God, deep down,
I want the bungalow.

Ta-hi-ti

Ta-hi-ti
Tahiti
Sheer abandon
and promise -
wrecked on her walls of coral,
destitute on her shores…
the boat that rocks
and the rocks that boat;
I beat them.
I made it.
In this aberration on centre earth -
the pebble in Pacific's pouch:
the one, not only,
but special.

At all sides, at sandhooked edges,
a friend, a shock of constance,
open sky, open mind,
free of the touches of man's mongering,
the creak-creak of journeying,
the waiting, the wanting:
the saddle of knowing
like the drip-drip of the incessant bathroom tap
or the residue of honey after pouring.

It is clean here, it is colourful here,
glamouring centuries of harnessed colony,
still unfree its progeny
but a holding dock
for my wreck
whilst I prepare to take to waves again.

ONCE-JOINED PIECES **159**

She is alluring, inviting
a place at her table.
I sit on the floor;
that is all I am able.
In this haven on my endless ocean
my eyes are lustred upon
ideas and intentions
far beyond my station,
for she warms the cold
and delivers sensation.
She wants little but what I offer:
opportunity to tell her story,
to tie ribbons on my mast.
But mostly, her golden sands
want for my far-strewn effects
to fold under:
to remain.
Island that once was joined,
brokered in harmony.
Remembrances -
to send white-winged doves
with sweet entreaty
to the land of darkness
I escaped.

stationary

steady rocks;
I'll be there forever for you, she says
under the patchwork sky
I stroke the surface, bubbling
paint streams to her timbre,
mellow and lilting
she always has words for me
and it kills me, knowing
where made of clay we moulded
and decided to make whole arms
just for us, that I had none but her
sail hoisted on the mast.
what is time when horizons are without
endings?
when wind is air that is moving?

bells rendering us stationary
never saw us here,
but we did.
ride with me, my silence bears;
I may never be the same
but I cast the line now
and I look for her
I know the frames are empty,
corners come sharp,
but she knows my fingers when they write -
she gave me my heart.
said "give it care,
give it doors and fashion keys
whilst I sew the stars there,":

ONCE-JOINED PIECES 161

for her, anything.
rain and sweet petrichor,
islands vim,
for her, give this:
clouds everywhere
on atmospheres thin
steady rocks as they take you in,
my arms on a lifetime,
still circling -
our whole world patient,
waiting for wind.

passage

I feel like the people of the cave
waking from a two hundred year slumber,
to see the fabric of the universe
unravelled and rolled up like thread on a folded paper.
A world that they thought they knew
risen from the collapse of all reason.
A blink of an eye, but in reality a passage
of worlds not determinable.
A dream in which I witnessed my own death,
and so long believed it to be so.
Truths ingrained in the very essence of my being
bleed out of my hands –
my blood is not blue, I learn;
and I am -
not you.

escalator girl

You are waves -
tsunami towers.
You are boundless.
You are heartbroken, confused, adrift.
You are gasping for breath, wave after wave
swung by the ankle across the room
You are rushing, anchors sinking like milk teeth in dragon-
scales
so tough it is to stop.
You are kind - you are trying to contend kindly with
difficulty
but anger is ragged, and loss is not a bucket you can fill
again.
You are mistakes - escalator mistakes.
One step, one rope, one anchor pulling up again.
You are so much more
than what your wounds suggest.
You get up again,
you smile again,
you try again.
The picture frames on the walls are not stuck there with glue
but you are walls
for nails to break through.
You are love - you love like an everflowing river
that weeps from your soul,
and you can love harder, faster, than you've ever been told.
You can, and you should, and you will, you have stood
on the shoulders of noone:
an empty space.
You have made living a beauty:
a hard-fought craze,

and let it be known far and wide
you are freedom's face.
You are so much more powerful than you know,
escalator girl;
you are not lost.
I carry you with me.

window sill

I was lucky, when sitting in window sills was an option,
hiding was easier;
I drew the curtains
and stared the short distance to
Ground,
considered momentum
and my most weightless form
holding each shard in my palm.

I was young, too young to know
too old to show
the tears, the fears
young enough for faults
to be my own
for dazzling illusions of hope
that I was just small.

I was the glue, the flag begrudged
with holding ceasefire
armed to the teeth
yet wielding no weapon
tasked and upholstered
agreement for all
I glued my nose to the window
and I knew war.

I was the piece, the weakest link
I fancied my destiny to sink
one day,
blameless like a feather
at the end of my tether

the ghost in the mirror
falling from the tree
but falling was not falling
It was never for free.

I was blue, in all its shades
blue like the carpet I cried against
quicksand footsteps along a blue edge
quiet to count dwindling breaths
blue like the blue of the ocean
I found myself forever lost in
blue for my own condemning
blue that I had always been dreading.

I was the fish, the flailing fish
on the end of the line
thrashing from left to right
railing against my rising tide
up, 10,000 feet
and down, down
river eyes meet
condensation
hand against the glass
I was sorry,
I was asked.

I was young, I was glue,
I was piece, I was blue
I was toy, I was plate
I was lost, I was freight
I was up, I was down

I was swung round and round
I was fish in the water
not enough to have caught her
I was window latch
I was double glaze
I was one small match
from the final blaze
I was pals with the demons
because I had to keep them
I was everything I needed
I was everything I did.
I was so alone, back then
I was so alone, back when
I was hiding on window sills,
dreaming of Ground
and not of Sky, for
what was closer?

fear was my boat
my rolling engine
now I am boat
I am momentum
even now I am fearsome
in my will to find
the answer.

ONCE-JOINED PIECES 169

170 ONCE-JOINED PIECES

Acknowledgements

All praise belongs to almighty Allah. This book has been an intensive labour of self-exploration and acceptance. The journey is not over – it never is. But I am so grateful for its beginning.

My parents have fought tirelessly for my education and career, and to them I am forever indebted. May Allah grant them a long and happy life. I am especially thankful to my brothers, who are the lights of my life. They make me better, just by existing. I hope that I can make them both proud.

Holly Winter-Hughes makes me wonder…is she an angel in disguise? She is kind and understanding from the deepest of places, and it is because of her that this book exists. Holly – thank you for your immense support over the last few years. I never quite dreamed this would be possible, but your belief in me has made it possible. Thank you to you, Gez and The Word Association for buoying my words to the surface.

Without the support of my teachers Emily Oram and Jacquie Reid, I would never have put my words out there for the world to see. You both drew out my passion and determination. I cannot thank you enough for the moments in which you saw me and nurtured me to where I am.

I want to give special thanks to Polly Smith, who was my therapist when I began to write this book. Polly – thank you for helping me swim. You listened to early versions of some of these poems and told me how important my words were. I will never forget your kindness and compassion, and the path through the pain that you helped me begin to build.

I owe a lot to my therapy family: Bryony, Anne-Marie, Kit and Zoe. I am never fighting alone because you have all held me with infinite care and strength. You have given me hope, helped me breathe, and enabled me to stand up long enough to write this book. It is my privilege to call you friends for life.

I wish I could thank each and every person who has given me strength and impetus to write this book. Thank you to my friends, colleagues, and mentors who I have not mentioned here. I am so grateful for your support (especially Phoebe – friend, colleague, and self-proclaimed publicist).

To Ayesha, Eleanor, Ieva, Nathan, Glory, Felicity and Becca – thank you each for your unwavering support and kindness. Each of your friendships has been anchoring in the most turbulent of times.

To my dear friends Becs, Zainäb, Harriet and Grace – thank you for the ocean of safety and hope you have given me.